The Fantastic Phonics Food Factory

Teacher/Parent Activity Guidebook

Shar Wilkes

Jane Grogan

Glenbridge Publishing Ltd.

Illustrations
Patricia Hobbs

Library of Congress Catalog Card Number: LC 99-97290

International Standard Book Number: 0-944435-48-3

ACKNOWLEDGMENTS

The evolvement of this program would not have been possible without the consistent and enthusiastic support of the administration of the Natrona County School District and the support of the many parents who experienced the joy of "learning to read" along with their children.

As most teachers will gratefully acknowledge, we owe a significant debt to our young students who have taught us so much.

There are too many individuals who encouraged us to expand and create this book to mention by name, but they must know of the deep appreciation we feel. But we would be remiss if we did not acknowledge the unstinting time and support of Amy Schicketanz, computer expert and parent, Stan Olson, Superintendent of Schools, Casper, Wyoming, and our own children for their help and support for the creation of *The Fantastic Phonics Food Factory*.

INTRODUCTION

The program you are about to explore is designed to help students experience the sounds of the English language through a multi-modality approach, which incorporates all of the senses. We encourage new processing techniques to enhance the creative learning channels. The use of humor makes the experience delightful and fun. Diverse memory games are used to reinforce memorization of the sounds. These same techniques are replicated and reinforced while teaching the initial sound blending techniques.

In Part One the teacher or parent reads the book to the children to familiarize them with the characters. All characters are introduced at the same time, and charts showing the characters should be placed on walls in the classroom. Then, the actual teaching of each phoneme begins. After introducing each letter and sound the teacher or parent will wish to spend at least fifteen minutes reinforcing the letter and sound by having the child write both upper and lower case letters and saying the letter name and sound as he writes. Each student should have a composition book or journal in which to write. After the children have written the letter and sound, practiced them, and the concept is firm, they may draw a picture of the character in the upper right-hand corner of the page.

Each character of the program is a food. The ultimate reinforcement to learning the sound is to "eat a word." The students soon come to know and love each sound. The characters have their own "charade" also. Games, such as charading a word, are fun for the child and also offer a strong reinforcement to learning the sounds. The charade and other activities are explained in each section of the *Guidebook*. A list of charades may be found in Appendix A.

Teaching reading through the arts has opened up new and creative channels to reinforce the learning of these characters. Sculpting a character as each sound is learned is a good way to strengthen the letter and sound connection and is an important activity in this method. Connecting the sound association with the action of the character is the secret. When the sculpted characters are arranged to make words, reading begins with comfort and delight.

Turning the characters into jewelry and/or painting a word are also great reinforcers, such as Beautiful Banana earrings or Dancing Doughnut pins and/or magnets. As the characters are sculpted or painted, they should be placed into a treasure chest that the child has made and decorated. When all the characters are learned, the children will recognize the treasure as their ability to read or write most words in the English language.

Writing adventure stories about the characters with beginning, middle, and end also makes the learning process exciting. Let the children make up stories about Beautiful Banana coming home from school, going to the park on Saturday morning, or playing on a swing and slide. Dancing Doughnut could audition for a career in a television commercial or be a member of a ballet troupe, with an explanation about the art form from the teacher or parent.

In Part Two, the Fantastic Phonics Food Factory characters are paraded to the factory. As they approach, they hear sounds coming from the factory. They hear sounds like "Ow! Oo! Aw!" As they enter, they are greeted by Shivering Shake saying "Sh. There are shenanigans going on in there." There is a food fight when the rest of the forty-five phonemes are introduced. They begin to slide into other characters, and as they do, they begin to form words.

Special Note:

Technically, phonemic sounds should be produced as a single sound. In the presentation of this text, however, the phoneme is represented with an exaggerated pronunciation to assist the presenter with the correct sound production. In the initial delivery of the lesson this is critical. However, as the presenter becomes more proficient with the method of presentation, the sounds will become much easier to manipulate and should become a single sound, i.e., "cuh" would become "c." The attached phoneme may then be dropped. We are not using the letter names of the consonants, only the long vowel sounds.

Alliteration technique is used throughout the program to reinforce the sound. The character names and story lines all reinforce this concept.

Part One

Meet the Fantastic Phonics A–Z

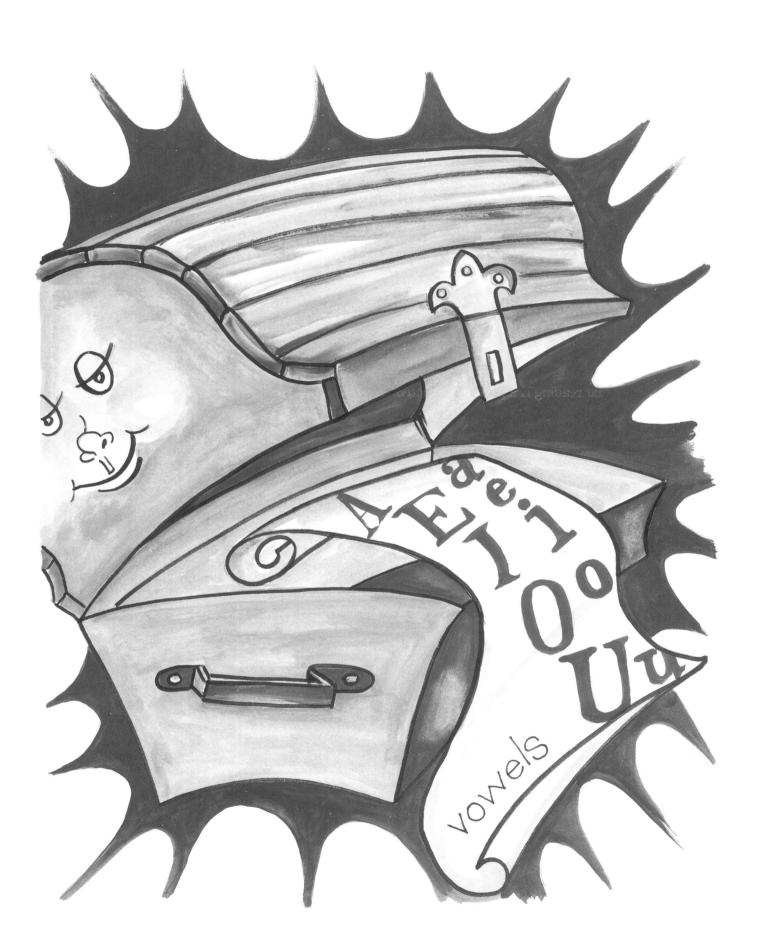

PROJECTS

Your imagination in developing materials is the key. Wall charts are essential. All characters should be displayed if possible. Some of the suggestions are more suitable for school settings. Others can be used both at home and/or school. Here are a few suggestions:

1. Produce bulletin board figures of the characters.

2. Create magnetic and/or flannel cutouts of the characters.

3. Use wooden cutout figures of the characters to decorate the school hallways.

4. Use overhead transparencies of the characters.

5. Cut paper dolls of the characters. Outfits designed by the children foster their creativity.

6. Make a treasure chest and sculpt a set of characters.

7. Create name tags using the characters.

8. Make puppets of the characters and put on puppet shows to foster more creativity and constructive playacting.

9. Create special character costumes as an art project, an opportunity to work with the art teacher.

10. Create a cookbook using the food characters.

11. Make up songs using the characters. The music teacher could aid in this project.

12. Compete with other classrooms using the newly learned reading skills.

13. Encourage projects that include parents as well as the children.

SHOPPING LIST
(Substitutions are fine)

Apples

Bananas

Carrots

Doughnuts

Eggs

Fish (crackers)

Gumdrops

Hot Dogs

Carbonated drink

Gummy Worms (Inedible Insects)

Jellybeans

Kiwi

Lemonade

Mushrooms

Noodles

Olives

Popcorn

Quivering Quake Cereal (invent)

Raisins

Sundaes

Tomatoes

Upside-Down Cake

Veggies

Waffles (waffle crisp cereal)

Yams

Zucchini

Shakes

Cherries

Frosting in a tube (Oodles of Ooze)

Oreo Cookies

Sprinkles

Artichokes

Wheat Crackers

Dressing

Smoked Oysters

Thermos filled with punch

Spice (Ounces of Ouch)

Allspice

Treats in a Treasure Chest

5 jars of cookie dough

Dough bowls for long vowels

SECRET INGREDIENTS

The ingredients of the Fantastic Phonics Food Factory are the character names and sounds of the alphabet. They are secret since the children do not know them yet. They will learn them through identification with foods, some of which may be their favorites.

1. You will wish to memorize the character names and sounds. The characters A through Z are presented in alphabetical order. All the other characters are also phoneme sounds of the English language.

2. Short vowel sounds are included in the A–Z category. They are to be taught by their sounds rather than their letter names.

3. Long vowel sounds are taught separately at the end of the lessons. They are taught using their letter names (a, e, i, o, u).

4. Each letter has a character and mnemonic device incorporated with its personality to help use association to facilitate memory of names and sounds.

5. Some learning modalities include: auditory, visual, "eat a word," "smell a word," "charade a word," "paint a word," and "sculpt a word." Children may be encouraged to exercise their creativity to devise other modalities that may work for them. Suggestions for teachers and parents are included in the previous section.

6. Jars on a shelf may be used to teach words with the same sounds but with alternative spellings. Word lists appear throughout the *Guidebook* for your convenience. The teacher should select words that are in the vocabularies of the children and will depend upon the abilities of the children. A number of words used in this text will require an explanation, however. The teacher should focus on success.

7. Have the children sculpt each character as you proceed through the stories. The children should save the set of characters, and as they progress through the program, they can begin to form words using the sculpted characters.

8. Since the sounds represent food, the children can "eat the sounds" as they "travel" along the reading pathways.

CHARACTER LIST

Aa	Antsy Apple
Bb	Beautiful Banana
Cc	Cool Carrot
Dd	Dancing Doughnut
Ee	Entertaining Eggs
Ff	Fancy Fish
Gg	Galloping Gumdrop
Hh	Hammering Hot Dog
Ii	Inedible Insects
Jj	Juggling Jellybeans
Kk	King Kiwi
Ll	Leaping Lemonade
Mm	Muscular Mushroom
Nn	Napping Noodle
Oo	Ominous Olives
Pp	Popping Popcorn
Qq	Quivering Quake
Rr	Racing Raisin
Ss	Singing Sundae
Tt	Tumbling Tomato
Uu	Upside-Down Cake
Vv	Vested Vegetables
Ww	Wallowing Waffles
Xx	X-soda
Yy	Yodeling Yams
Zz	Zipping Zucchini

Combinations

Ss	Treasure Chest
Sh	Shivering Shake
Ch	Chattering Cherries
OO	Oodles of Ooze
Ar	Artistic Artichoke
Th	Then there were thousands — thousands of things
oo	Ooookie Cookie
Oy	Oysters
Wh	Whining Wheat Cracker
Ou	Ounces of Ouch
Th	Thirsty Thermos
∂	Miss Schwa
Aw	Awful Allspice
Ng	Dripping Dressing

Long A
Long E
Long I
Long O
Long U

SECRET PASSAGES

As you and your students proceed through the different sounds and characters, allow them the opportunity to create their own adventures.

Sculpt the characters as they are introduced to reinforce the sounds the characters make. Sculpt a treasure chest large enough for all the characters (or use a milk carton that the children can decorate) and put the sculpted characters into the treasure chest. Remove them as you introduce sound blending and as you and the children begin to form words. After words have been formed successfully, sentences may then be introduced.

The treasure chest secret is simply that once the child knows all the sounds, he may learn to "sound blend," a process that allows the child to read and write most words of the English language. The children can then appreciate the wonderful treasure they have discovered.

LONG VOWEL SOUNDS

The long vowels are: **A, E, I, O, U,** and sometimes **Y.** The long vowels always say their names. **Y** is usually a consonant sound saying "yuh," but in certain word formations the **Y** can say a long **E** or a long **I,** or other sounds. **Y** will appear as the long vowel sound such as in the word "my."

The concept taught in this program is that the short vowel sounds are introduced with all the other phonemes in the language. The long vowels are formed when joined with other sounds of the language, and their spellings are dependent on where they are placed in the words they represent. Therefore, "jars on the shelf" become very important to separate the different spellings, and quite frequently memorization is the best tool for retaining the correct spelling.

SOUND BLENDING TECHNIQUES

Teacher/Parent Directives

Teacher: Insert the magical key and let our adventures begin. Listen carefully. It's time to sound blend a word. Cool Carrot (teacher may act out [charade] by snapping fingers).

Student: **C** ("cuh")

Teacher: Antsy Apple (charade by brushing off ants)

Student: **A** ("ah")

Teacher: Beautiful banana (charade by bouncing a ball)

Student: **B** ("buh")

Teacher: Say it all together: **C - A - B.** Say it fast . . . **CAB.** Great job!
(Teacher may make circular motion with hand indicating to the children to "say it fast.")
The teacher may hold up index finger to represent "cuh," the next finger to represent "ah," and the third finger to represent "buh" with spaces between the fingers. The teacher may then place these three fingers together to illustrate to the children that the three letters are to be thought of together to spell "cab."

THE ADVENTURE TO END ALL ADVENTURES

An excellent way to review at any time after the characters, sounds, and names have been introduced is to have each child bring the food of a different sound. Cut the foods up into tiny pieces and let the students experiment by making words with the foods. You will find short, one-syllable words will grow into four- to five-syllable words for the opportunity to increase the number of foods the children get to eat. This may very likely be their favorite activity!

Read the following to the children:

"Welcome to the Fantastic Phonics Food Factory! You are about to begin a great adventure. You will meet the 45 fantastic phonics and you will want to remember their names and sounds. We want you to have fun and, at the same time, you might find a treasure waiting for you!"

ANTSY APPLE

Read the Story

Our first fantastic phonic for you to meet is Antsy Apple! Antsy Apple fell out of his apple tree one day and found ants all over him! As he anxiously brushed them off, all he could aptly say was,
"a . . . a . . . a . . . a . . . a . . ."
(ah) (ah) (ah) (ah) (ah)

Projects

- Charade the sound by using hands to brush off the ants. The children may sculpt the character very small giving it eyes and mouth. Insert a pencil or toothpick into the mouth to show him saying "a . . . a . . . a"

- Provide an apple treat for the children.

Mnemonic Devices

Memory games include "eating" a word, charading a word, sculpting a word, and/or sniffing a word. The other sounds must be taught prior to using this technique.

For the sound "an," say: "Antsy Apple/Napping Noodle." Do not tell the children the word. Have them sound blend and realize the word on their own. The same technique will be used throughout the entire program.

Mnemonic Reading and Writing, Sculpting, Charading, and Painting

1. An: Antsy Apple, Napping Noodle.
2. Ant: Antsy Apple, Napping Noodle, Tumbling Tomato.
3. At: Antsy Apple, Tumbling Tomato.
4. Ask: Antsy Apple, Singing Sundae, King Kiwi.
5. Cab: Cool Carrot, Antsy Apple, Beautiful Banana.
6. Can: Cool Carrot, Antsy Apple, Napping Noodle.
7. Bat: Beautiful Banana, Antsy Apple, Tumbling Tomato.
8. Rat: Racing Raisins, Antsy Apple, Tumbling Tomato.
9. Dad: Dancing Doughnut, Antsy Apple, Dancing Doughnut.
10. Man: Muscular Mushroom, Antsy Apple, Napping Noodle.

Three Jars on the Shelf

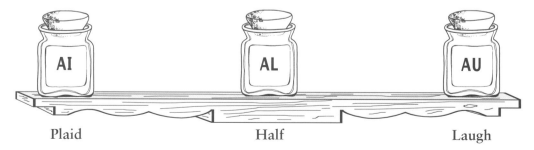

Plaid   Half   Laugh

The above show letter combinations that are pronounced "a" (ah) but have different spellings. Children may be introduced to these different spellings when they are ready.

BEAUTIFUL BANANA

Read the Story

Beautiful Banana was invited to be "Miss Banana" of Fantastic Phonics Land because of her boundless beauty! As she walked briskly on stage bouncing her ball, all you could brilliantly hear was,
"b . . . b . . . b . . . b . . . b . . ."
(buh) (buh) (buh) (buh) (buh)

Projects

- Demonstrate the action of a bouncing ball
- Follow the same mnemonic devices used previously
- Auditory memory games — "eat" a word, charade a word
- Sculpt the Beautiful Banana character
- Sniff a word, and/or eat a banana treat
- Sculpt Beautiful Banana and place her in the decorated milk carton treasure chest

Timed reading lists are very effective techniques. The children can play "beat the clock." To assist the children in the formation of the letters **b** and **d** ask them to hold up their hands and place their outstretched thumbs together holding their other fingers straight up in the air. They will make the shape of a bed with their hands. Tell them this is a good memory device if they forget which direction **b,** or **d** faces. The mnemonic clue is the shape of a "bed" made with the thumbs touching. Since some children will experience reversal problems with these letters, this will help them.

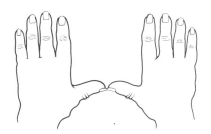

Mnemonic Reading and Writing, Sculpting, Charading, and Painting

1. Bad: Beautiful Banana, Antsy Apple, Dancing Doughnut.
2. Bed: Beautiful Banana, Entertaining Eggs, Dancing Doughnut.
3. Bag: Beautiful Banana, Antsy Apple, Galloping Gumdrop.
4. Bug: Beautiful Banana, UpsideDown Cake, Galloping Gumdrop.
5. Bit: Beautiful Banana, Inedible Insects, Tumbling Tomato.
6. But: Beautiful Banana, Upside-Down Cake, Tumbling Tomato.
7. Bun: Beautiful Banana, Upside-Down Cake, Napping Noodle.
8. Bob: Beautiful Banana, Ominous Olives, Beautiful Banana.
9. Pub: Popping Popcorn, Upside-Down Cake, Beautiful Banana.
10. Dab: Dancing Doughnut, Antsy Apple, Beautiful Banana.

Dictation Sentences

1. Bob had a big bug.
2. He had it in a bag.

Cool Carrot

Read the Story

Cool Carrot was clearly the coolest dude in Fantastic Phonics Land! He was constantly walking around carefully snapping his fingers and calmly singing, "I'm so cool"!

"c . . . c . . . c . . . c . . . c . . ."
(cuh) (cuh) (cuh) (cuh) (cuh)

Projects

- Charade the sound by snapping fingers and prancing proudly around the room
- Eat a carrot treat
- Charade a cool carrot. (As before, alternative spellings of a sound are located as jars on the shelf. You can use baby food jars for jars on the shelf.)

If a particular word is being used and not included in the jars, just add the extra jar as needed. Cool Carrot has three jars on the shelf. The two alternative spellings are: "k" and "ck."

Three Jars on the Shelf

c	K	ck
Cat	Kin	Back
Cot	King	Sack
Cut	Kid	Tack

Mnemonic Reading and Writing, Sculpting, Charading, and Painting

1. Can: Cool Carrot, Antsy Apple, Napping Noodle. (The children can guess the word.)
2. Cup: Cool Carrot, Upside-Down Cake, Popping Popcorn.
3. Cut: Cool Carrot, Upside-Down Cake, Tumbling Tomato.
4. Cub: Cool Carrot, Upside-Down Cake, Beautiful Banana.
5. Cash: Cool Carrot, Antsy Apple, Shivering Shake.
6. Clip: Cool Carrot, Leaping Lemonade, Inedible Insects, Popping Popcorn.
7. Clap: Cool Carrot, Leaping Lemonade, Antsy Apple, Popping Popcorn.
8. Club: Cool Carrot, Leaping Lemonade, Upside-Down Cake, Beautiful Banana.
9. Cat: Cool Carrot, Antsy Apple, Tumbling Tomato.
10. Cap: Cool Carrot, Antsy Apple, Popping Popcorn.

A "k" Sound Spelled "ck."

1. Pack: Popping Popcorn, Antsy Apple, Cool Carrot (spelled "ck.")
2. Pick: Popping Popcorn, Inedible Insects, Cool Carrot (spelled "ck.")
3. Tack: Tumbling Tomato, Antsy Apple, Cool Carrot.
4. Back: Beautiful Banana, Antsy Apple, Cool Carrot.
5. Lick: Leaping Lemonade, Inedible Insects, Cool Carrot.

Note: "ck" is used at the end of a short one-syllable word that contains a short vowel sound in the position preceding the "ck."

DANCING DOUGHNUT

Read the Story

Dancing Doughnut is our darling fantastic phonic! He dances nights at the dance hall. He also deftly sings ditties on the radio for the dramatic disc jockey. The jingles always start out the same,
"d . . . d . . . d . . . d . . . d . . ."
(duh) (duh) (duh) (duh) (duh)

Projects

- Eat a doughnut
- Charade a doughnut by moving arms and hands as if dancing
- Sculpt a doughnut and place in the treasure chest

Mnemonic Reading and Writing, Sculpting, Charading, and Painting

1. Dab: Dancing Doughnut, Antsy Apple, Beautiful Banana.
2. Dad: Dancing Doughnut, Antsy Apple, Dancing Doughnut.
3. Den: Dancing Doughnut, Entertaining Eggs, Napping Noodle.
4. Dug: Dancing Doughnut, Upside-Down Cake, Galloping Gumdrop.
5. Dig: Dancing Doughnut, Inedible Insects, Galloping Gumdrop.
6. Dot: Dancing Doughnut, Ominous Olives, Tumbling Tomato.
7. Duck: Dancing Doughnut, Upside-Down Cake, Cool Carrot (spelled "ck").
8. Dim: Dancing Doughnut, Inedible Insects, Muscular Mushroom.

ENTERTAINING EGGS

Read the Story

Entertaining Eggs are an excellent part of the dance team! Entertaining Eggs are enthusiastic every day! They are a little "egg" centric and are known for keeping their sunny side up and saying,

"e . . . e . . . e . . . e . . . e . . ."
(eh) (eh) (eh) (eh) (eh)

Projects

- Charade the character by flipping your hand, palm side up
- Sculpt the character
- Try a puppet show with the children making up the story

Seven Jars on the Shelf (short "E" sound)

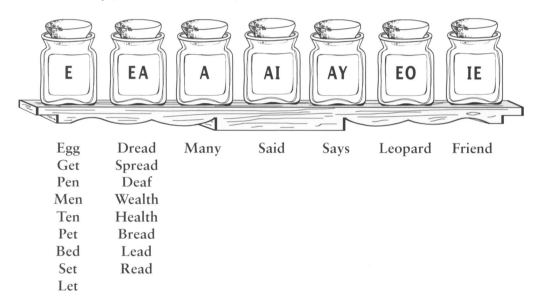

E	EA	A	AI	AY	EO	IE
Egg	Dread	Many	Said	Says	Leopard	Friend
Get	Spread					
Pen	Deaf					
Men	Wealth					
Ten	Health					
Pet	Bread					
Bed	Lead					
Set	Read					
Let						

Dictation

Ten pets get the bed.

Mnemonic Reading and Writing, Sculpting, Charading, and Painting

1. Egg: Entertaining Eggs, Galloping Gumdrop (spelled "gg").
2. Get: Galloping Gumdrop, Entertaining Eggs, Tumbling Tomato.
3. Pen: Popping Popcorn, Entertaining Eggs, Napping Noodle.
4. Men: Muscular Mushroom, Entertaining Eggs, Napping Noodle.
5. Ten: Tumbling Tomato, Entertaining Eggs, Napping Noodle.
6. Pet: Popping Popcorn, Entertaining Eggs, Tumbling Tomato.
7. Bed: Beautiful Banana, Entertaining Eggs, Dancing Doughnut.

8. Set: Singing Sundae, Entertaining Eggs, Tumbling Tomato.
9. Let: Leaping Lemonade, Entertaining Eggs, Tumbling Tomato.

Mnemonic Reading and Writing, Sculpting, Charading, and Painting for Short "E" Spelled "EA"

1. Read: Racing Raisins, Entertaining Eggs (spelled "ea"), Dancing Doughnut.
2. Lead: Leaping Lemonade, Entertaining Eggs (spelled "ea"), Dancing Doughnut.
3. Deaf: Dancing Doughnut, Entertaining Eggs (spelled "ea"), Fancy Fish.
4. Health: Hammering Hot Dog, Entertaining Eggs (spelled "ea"), Leaping Lemonade, Thirsty Thermos.
5. Bread: Beautiful Banana, Racing Raisin, Entertaining Eggs (spelled "ea"), Dancing Doughnut.
6. Spread: Singing Sundae, Popping Popcorn, Racing Raisin, Entertaining Eggs (spelled "ea"), Dancing Doughnut.

FANCY FISH

Read the Story

Fancy Fish lives in a fancy fishbowl! He likes to flutter his fins. He is a fantastic flipper and is known for his five mile finish! These days, as he swims around his fishbowl, one can hear him fluttering,
"f . . . f . . . f . . . f . . . f . . ."
(fuh) (fuh) (fuh) (fuh) (fuh)

Projects

- Charade the sound by showing how a fish swims, making a fluttering movement with the hands
- Sculpt a fish and use cutouts
- Make up good fish stories

Four Jars on the Shelf

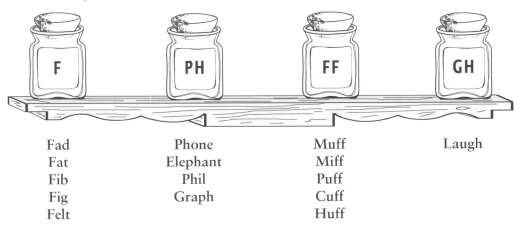

F	PH	FF	GH
Fad	Phone	Muff	Laugh
Fat	Elephant	Miff	
Fib	Phil	Puff	
Fig	Graph	Cuff	
Felt		Huff	

Dictation

He had a fat fig and felt fit.

Mnemonic Reading and Writing, Sculpting, Charading, and Painting

1. Fad: Fancy, Fish, Antsy apple, Dancing Doughnut.
2. Fat: Fancy Fish, Antsy Apple, Tumbling Tomato.
3. Felt: Fancy Fish, Entertaining Eggs, Leaping Lemonade, Tumbling Tomato.
4. Graph: Galloping Gumdrop, Racing Raisins, Antsy Apple, Fancy Fish (spelled "ph").
5. Laugh: Leaping Lemonade, Antsy Apple (spelled "au"), Fancy Fish (spelled "gh").
6. Puff: Popping Popcorn, Upside-Down Cake, Fancy Fish (spelled "ff").

Another Little Secret

Short words ending in **f, l, s**, usually double the last letter. (They look like twins!)

Muff	Buff	Doll	Spell	Mess	Miss
Miff	Huff	Spill	Sell	Fuss	Russ
Puff		Tell		Grass	

GALLOPING GUMDROP

Read the Story

Galloping Gumdrop always has a great time! He gallops from gate to gate greeting good girls and boys. As he gallops he always greets everyone and says, "Giddy-up!"

"g . . . g . . . g . . . g . . . g . . ."
(guh) (guh) (guh) (guh) (guh)

Projects

- Charade the character by pretending to be on a horse holding reins
- Eat a gumdrop for a treat
- Try a cutout of this character

Word List

1. Gig	3. Get	5. Gag	7. Go
2. Gab	4. Gad	6. Gas	8. Gift

Dictation

1. Go get the gas.
2. It is a gag gift!

HAMMERING HOT DOG

Read the Story

Hammering Hot Dog is a hard worker. He hammers all day and hammers all night. He has a hard life! Hammering is a hard job! Late at night you can hear Hammering Hot Dog happily saying,
"h . . . h . . . h . . . h . . . h . . ."
(huh) (huh) (huh) (huh) (huh)

Projects

- Charade the sound by pretending to hammer a nail
- The children could eat a meat stick for a treat
- Cut out letters to make words
- Sculpt the sound for the treasure chest

Word List

1.	Hat	6.	Hut
2.	Had	7.	Head
3.	Hot	8.	Hand
4.	Him	9.	Ham
5.	Hit	10.	Hum

Dictation

He had a hit.
He can hum.

INEDIBLE INSECTS

Read the Story

Isabel is intimidated by the inedible insects she was served for lunch! As she runs away, all she can say is, icky, icky. She would rather have immense cupcakes instead.
"i . . . i . . . i . . . i . . . i . . ."
(ih) (ih) (ih) (ih) (ih)

Projects

- Charade the sound by pushing away from a plate saying
  "i . . . i . . . i . . . i . . . i . . ."
- Eat a "Gummy Worm" for a treat
- Make up stories about foods the children do not like

Five Jars on the Shelf

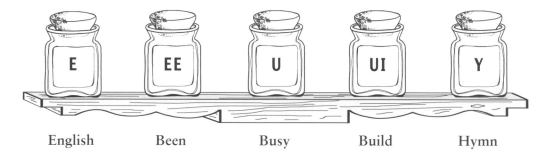

English   Been   Busy   Build   Hymn

Word List

1. Hit
2. Dig
3. Him
4. Lid
5. Dim

6. Did
7. It
8. Lit
9. Tim
10. Hid

Dictation

It is lit.
Did it fit him? (Introduce the concept of a question.)

JUGGLING JELLYBEAN

Read the Story

Juggling Jellybean is a jingling juggler. Juggling Jellybean juggles just for kids. As Juggling Jellybean juggles, he always has fun. You can just hear him juggling from far away.

"j . . . j . . . j . . . j . . . j . . ."
(juh) (juh) (juh) (juh) (juh)

Projects

• Demonstrate to the class how one would juggle
• Say "j . . . j . . . j . . ."
• Have a jellybean
• Charade the sound by juggling in the air
• Sculpt the sound
• Review the contents of the treasure chests

Five Jars on the Shelf

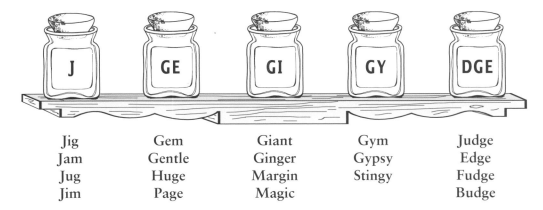

J	GE	GI	GY	DGE
Jig	Gem	Giant	Gym	Judge
Jam	Gentle	Ginger	Gypsy	Edge
Jug	Huge	Margin	Stingy	Fudge
Jim	Page	Magic		Budge

Dictation

Jim hid the jam.

Another Secret Ingredient

E, I, and **Y,** melt hard sounds into soft sounds. If **G** or **C** are followed by **E, I,** or **Y,** it will turn the hard sound soft most of the time.

G becomes a **J** sound; **C** becomes an **S** sound.

Mnemonic Reading and Writing, Sculpting, Charading, and Painting

1. Jet: Juggling Jellybean, Entertaining Eggs, Tumbling Tomato.
2. Jam: Juggling Jellybean, Antsy Apple, Muscular Mushroom.
3. Gem: Juggling Jellybean (spelled "g") Entertaining Eggs, Muscular Mushroom.
4. Gym: Juggling Jellybean (spelled "gy"), Muscular Mushroom.
5. Margin: Muscular Mushroom, Artistic Artichoke (spelled "ar"), Juggling Jellybean (spelled "gi"), Napping Noodle.
6. Judge: Juggling Jellybean, Upside-Down Cake, Juggling Jellybean (spelled "dge").

KING KIWI

Read the Story

King Kiwi was crowned "King of Soccer" this year for his great kick! You can hear King Kiwi in the yard practicing kicking for hours. King Kiwi also plays the kazoo.

"k . . . k . . . k . . . k . . . k . . ."
(kuh) (kuh) (kuh) (kuh) (kuh)

Projects

- Demonstrate a kick and say k . . . k . . . k . . .
- Charade the sound by making a kicking motion
- Have a Kiwi treat
- Make up a story about King Kiwi, which may include music. (King Kiwi has the same sound as Cool Carrot.)

Three Jars on the Shelf

Can	Kick	Sack
Cat	King	Duck
Cup	Kit	Tack

Dictation

A kid had a kit.

Mnemonic Reading and Writing, Sculpting, Charading, and Painting

1. Kid: King Kiwi, Inedible Insects, Dancing Doughnut.
2. Cup: Cool Carrot, Upside-Down Cake, Popping Popcorn.
3. Sock: Singing Sundae, Ominous Olives, King Kiwi (spelled "ck").
4. (On the final "ck" spelling either Cool Carrot or King Kiwi is correct. Say "ck.")

LEAPING LEMONADE

Read the Story

Leaping Lemonade was born in a blender. Leaping Lemonade loves lemons. She has spent her life listening to the lullabies and lulling. You can hear her leap by listening.
"l . . . l . . . l . . . l . . . l . . ."
   (əl)   (əl)   (əl)   (əl)(əl)

Projects

- Charade the sound by spreading arms as if leaping
- Improvise a circular blending motion with finger
- Children might enjoy leaping and "lulling"
- Have a glass of lemonade
- Cut out letters

- Sculpt the letter
- Say to the children: "Leaping Lemonade, Inedible Insects, Dancing Doughnut." See if they can say "Lid."

Three Jars on the Shelf

Lit	Stumble	Doll
Let	Jungle	Bell
Lot	Dazzle	Fell
Lab	Pimple	Yell
Lug	Sniffle	Hill

* Tell the children that the only place they will find Miss Schwa (∂) is in the dictionary. She is the upside-down "e."

Dictation

He left the lid off.

MUSCULAR MUSHROOM

Read the Story

Muscular Mushroom makes money lifting weights. Many say Muscular Mushroom is very muscular! When he makes his entrance, he moves his muscles and says,
"m . . . m . . . m . . . m . . . m . . ."

Projects

- Charade the character by having everyone show his/her muscles and say "mmmmm"
- Continue making the sculpted characters and putting them together to make words

Word List

1. Mom	3. Men	5. Mitt	7. Mess	9. Map
2. Man	4. Mop	6. Mutt	8. Mat	10. Mad

Dictation

Mop the mess on the mat.

NAPPING NOODLE

Read the Story

Napping Noodle naps not at nighttime! Napping Noodle naps all day until noon. Napping Noodle knows that too much napping isn't good, but nods off and snoozes just the same.

"n . . . n . . . n . . . n . . . n . . ."

Projects

- Charade the sound by putting your head to the side, close eyes, and say "nnnnn"
- Say: Napping Noodle, Antsy Apple, Popping Popcorn. What's the word? "nap"
- Eat a piece of red licorice spaghetti
- Make up stories about a Napping Noodle
- Sculpt the noodle for the treasure chest

Four Jars on the Shelf:

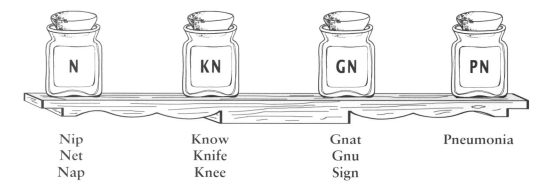

N	KN	GN	PN
Nip	Know	Gnat	Pneumonia
Net	Knife	Gnu	
Nap	Knee	Sign	

Dictation

The cat nods off and naps on the man.

OMINOUS OLIVES

Read the Story

Ominous Olives are known for their obvious outlook! See Oliver, optimistically holding on to an olive jar while his friend Oscar practices octaves for his visit to the opera.

"o . . . o . . . o . . . o . . . o . . ."

(aah) (aah) (aah) (aah) (aah)

Projects

- Charade the character by holding up your arm as if you are holding up a cape and say the sound "ooooo" (short "o"). Have the children imitate you

- Sing a musical scale to the sound of O
- Try to charade a whole word. First demonstrate Ominous Olive and then Napping Noodle to form the word "on"

One Jar on a Shelf

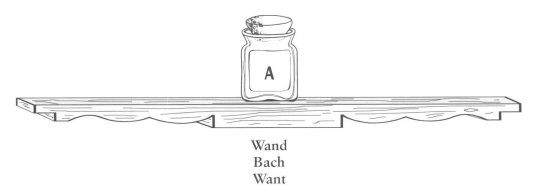

Wand
Bach
Want

Word List

1. On	3. Ron	5. Don	7. Lot	9. Drop
2. Con	4. Bon	6. Not	8. Spot	10. Top

POPPING POPCORN

Read the Story

Popping Popcorn is a people pleaser. Popping Popcorn walks around pleasing people by popping more popcorn for them. You can hear Popping Popcorn down the block — popping away.

"p . . . p . . . p . . . p . . . p . . ."
(puh) (puh) (puh) (puh) (puh)

Projects

- For a charade, the children may make popping effects with their fingers snapping in the air
- Sculpt the character for the treasure chest
- Make up stories about popcorn
- Eat some popcorn

Say: Popping Popcorn, Ominous Olive, Popping Popcorn. What's the word? "pop"

Word List

1. Cop	3. Pig	5. Pom-Pom	7. Pun	9. Pluck
2. Pad	4. Pod	6. Pot	8. Pat	

Dictation

Pat a pig and tap the tip.

QUIVERING QUAKE

Read the Story

Quivering Quake is great for a quick start in the morning! Some like to say, "quack, quack" as they eat Quivering Quake. It gives you such a quaint feeling. When you leave for school, you will be quietly saying, "quack! quack"! instead of a quick goodbye!

"qu . . . qu . . . qu . . . qu . . . qu . . ."
(kw)   (kw)   (kw)   (kw)   (kw)

Q never goes anywhere without his best friend **u**.

Projects

- Charade this character by shaking your hand in a quivering motion
- For a treat offer cereal and change the label to read "Quivering Quake"
- Sound blend this word: Quivering Quake, Inedible Insects, Cool Carrot — spelled "ck" or "Quick"

Word List

1. Quiz
2. Quit
3. Quip
4. Quiet
5. Quite

Dictation

He quit the quiz.

RACING RAISINS

Read the Story

Racing Raisins run races. The rule is to reach the finish line each race. Racing Raisins rarely rest! Racing Raisins are a rare breed. You must never be rude to a Racing Raisin! As they race, you can really hear them from far away.

"r . . . r . . . r . . . r . . . r . . ."
(ir)   (ir)   (ir)   (ir)   (ir)

Projects

- To charade this sound pretend you are a race car driver with your hand on the gear shift going "RRRRRR"
- Have a little box of raisins
- Sculpt the character

This is a difficult sound. It has many alternative spellings. We will demonstrate it with seven jars on the shelf.

Seven Jars on the Shelf

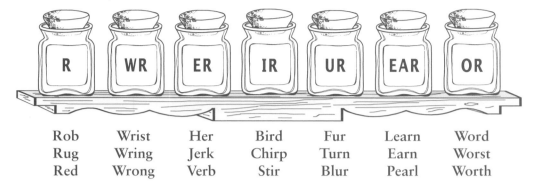

R	WR	ER	IR	UR	EAR	OR
Rob	Wrist	Her	Bird	Fur	Learn	Word
Rug	Wring	Jerk	Chirp	Turn	Earn	Worst
Red	Wrong	Verb	Stir	Blur	Pearl	Worth

When playing auditory memory games, say "Racing Raisin" and then give the appropriate spelling for the sound, i.e., Racing Raisin spelled "WR," Inedible Insects, Singing Sundae, Tumbling Tomato, spells "Wrist."

(*Special Note:* "or," "air," "ear," are not phonemes. They are two sounds put together. However, you may want to introduce them at this time.)

SINGING SUNDAE

Read the Story

Singing Sundae performs on Sundays! Singing Sundae sings and serves sirloins at the same time. As she sings, you can hear the sizzling sirloins she serves as they sizzle. "s . . . s . . . s . . . s . . . s . . ."

Projects

- Charade the sound by holding up your arm holding a pretend platter and say "SSSS"
- Prepare sundaes in the classroom
- Sculpt the character
- Make posters for the classroom wall

Four Jars on the Shelf

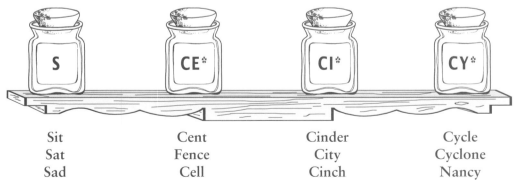

S	CE*	CI*	CY*
Sit	Cent	Cinder	Cycle
Sat	Fence	City	Cyclone
Sad	Cell	Cinch	Nancy

* "e, i, y" rule melts hard **c** to soft **c**.

Some examples of twins: Less, Fuss, Kiss, Mess, Chess.

Dictation

I sit in the sun and sip.

TUMBLING TOMATO

Read the Story

Tumbling Tomato has had a terrible time trying to tie her shoes! Each time she tries, she tumbles. In fact, we just heard her tumble off the table twice.
"t . . . t . . . t . . . t . . . t . . ."
(tuh) (tuh) (tuh) (tuh) (tuh)

Projects

- Charade the sound by pretending to start a cartwheel as if tumbling and saying "TTTT"
- Sculpt the character
- Tell stories about tumbling

Word List

1. Top	3. Tip	5. Tub	7. Tan	9. Tug
2. Tap	4. Ted	6. Tab	8. Tag	10. To

Dictation

Tap the ten tins.

UPSIDE-DOWN CAKE

Read the Story

Upside-Down Cake was in a terrible fix! Upside-Down Cake was utterly exhausted and fell. Unexpectedly, he raised his understandably unaccustomed arms. He was upset, and as he fell, all anyone could understand was,
"u . . . u . . . u . . . u . . . u . . ."
(uh) (uh) (uh) (uh) (uh)

Projects

- Say the **u** sound as the short **u** sound
- Charade the sound by putting your arms in the air and pretending to fall holding an umbrella and say "uuuu"
- Say: Upside-Down Cake, Popping Popcorn. What's the word? "up"

Word List

1. Up	3. Hug	5. Dug	7. Jug	9. Bump
2. Gum	4. Cut	6. Mud	8. Jump	10. Lump

Dictation

It went up, up, up!

Introduce the exclamation mark.

(**A, E, I, O, U,** alternative spellings are the ∂, "schwa.")

VESTED VEGETABLES

Read the Story

Vested Vegetables are a very exclusive bunch! Vested Vegetables create very vibrant vests. They have invested and now own very vital sports vehicles. Voom! Voom! Voom!

"v . . .v . . .v . . .v . . .v . . ."
(vuh) (vuh) (vuh) (vuh) (vuh)

Projects

- Demonstrate a race car going v-v-v-voom
- Charade the character by holding on to an imaginary vest
- Say: Vested Vegetables, Entertaining Eggs, Singing Sundae, Tumbling Tomato. What did you spell? v-e-s-t, "vest"
- Sculpt the character
- Make up stories about fast race cars

Word List

1. Van	6. Vest
2. Vim	7. Vans
3. Vet	8. Vats
4. Vat	9. Vets
5. Voom	10. Invest

("Invest" is a two-syllable word. Say the word and clap on each of the two syllables. A syllable is a "bite" or a puff of breath.)

Dictation

The van went v-v-v-voom!

WALLOWING WAFFLES

Read the Story

Wallowing Waffles wiggle and waggle and have a wonderful time! Wallowing Waffles went wading in a wonderful syrup and all you could hear was, "w . . . w . . . w . . . w . . . w . . ."
(wuh) (wuh) (wuh) (wuh) (wuh)

Projects

• Charade the sound by rotating your arms in the air in a splashing effect saying "wwww"
• Say: Wallowing Waffle, Entertaining Eggs, Tumbling Tomato. What word did you spell? "wet"

Word List

1. Web	3. Wet	5. With	7. Wed	9. Wish
2. Wig	4. Wit	6. Win	8. Went	10. Wash

Dictation

We wish to win!

X – SODA

Read the Story

X-Soda is the latest drink! You will never pour it down the sink! It's exciting! It's exhilarating! It's X-Soda!
"x . . . x . . . x . . . x . . . x . . ."
(ks)   (ks)   (ks)   (ks)   (ks)

Projects

• Charade X-Soda by pretending to open a pop-top can that goes, "ks, ks, ks"
• Say: Beautiful Banana, Ominous Olives, X-Soda. What's the word? "box"
• Sculpt the character
• Make up stories about pop-top cans

Word List

1. Fix	3. Ax	5. Wax	7. Tax	9. Six
2. Box	4. Fox	6. Ox	8. Nix	10. Lox

Dictation

The fox will fix the ox in the box.

YODELING YAMS

Read the Story

Yodeling Yams jammed on top of Yellow Mountain yesterday! The young town could hear their youthful yodeling, while playing with yo-yos. Yodelay-heehoo!

"y . . . y . . . y . . . y . . . y . . ."
(yuh) (yuh) (yuh) (yuh) (yuh)

Projects

- Say: Yodeling Yams, Entertaining Eggs, Singing Sundae. What's the word? "yes"
- Charade the character by putting your hand to your mouth and pretend to yodel
- Make up a short play about yo-yos
- Sculpt the character

Word List

1. Yes
2. Yam
3. Yet
4. Yak
5. You
6. Yo-Yo

Dictation

Yes, you do have a yo-yo!

ZIPPING ZUCCHINI

Read the Story

Zipping Zucchini is saying good night. His zipper goes "zzzzz." He zooms into bed and before you know it, zap, he's snoozing and dreaming about the zebra at the zoo.

"z . . . z . . . z . . z . . . z . . ."

Two Jars on the Shelf

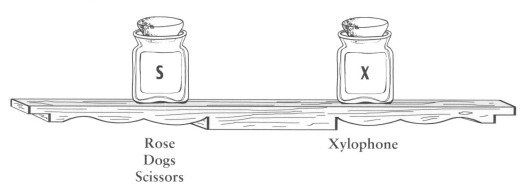

Rose
Dogs
Scissors

Xylophone

Projects

- Charade a zipper zipping
- Sculpt the character
- Tell zoo stories

Word List

1. Zoo
2. Zip
3. Zig-Zag
4. Zing
5. Whiz
6. Zap
7. Zeb
8. Zebra

Dictation

A zig-zag zip is in the zoo!

A MENU OF SIMPLE SIGHT WORDS

(Memorize the menu)

1. The
2. Of
3. Is
4. A
5. And
6. They
7. For
8. To
9. Do
10. From
11. Have
12. Was
13. What
14. You
15. Your

Part Two

The Food Fight!

PARADE DAY

Read the Story

It was parade day in Fantastic Phonics Land. All the phonics were so excited to be in the parade! Some of the phonics formed a line and started marching down to the food factory. They were to meet the rest of the phonics at the factory. They wanted to find the treasure chest! The phonics all chanted, "there's a measure of pleasure when we find the treasure, s . . . s . . . s . . . (zh . . . zh . . . zh). We want the treasure!" But all they heard was, "ow! oy! oo! aw!"

Projects

Have the children choose a character and make costumes and parade around making words. The **s** character is identified as the treasure chest, the **s** sound you hear in the middle of the word "treasure." Say "A measure of treasure." Identify the medial sound of **s**. The treasure chest is what is found after the phonics leave the factory.

They open the treasure chest and discover they can read and write most of the words in the English language because they have learned all the different sounds. What a wonderful treasure to find! As a follow-up activity, you can place all the words from the word lists into the treasure chest and roll them up like scrolls. Have the students unroll them and read them.

A scavenger hunt might be a great follow-up activity for more reading reinforcement. The **s** sound is charaded by the action of opening up the treasure chest. Say **s** as you open it. This is a very difficult sound and will need the necessary reinforcement. Fill the treasure chest with goodies for a treasure chest treat.

Two Jars on the Shelf

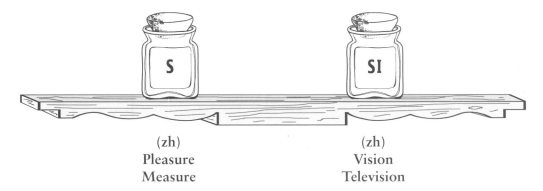

(zh)   (zh)
Pleasure   Vision
Measure   Television

At this point in the program it is a good time for evaluation. There are several ways to reinforce the sounds already introduced. One way is to flash the sounds in a flash card presentation format. If this skill is mastered, follow the same procedure using only the letter symbol. When the students know the correct sounds of all the letters, dictate the sounds in isolation and evaluate if they can correctly reproduce the written letters for the sounds. Tell the children that once they know all the sounds, the parade procession can enter the food factory.

SHIVERING SHAKE

Read the Story

As the Fantastic Phonics march to the factory, they are greeted by Shivering Shake saying, there are shenanigans going on!
"sh . . . sh . . . sh . . . sh . . . sh . . ."

Projects

* Charade the character by putting your index finger to your lips and saying "sh"
* Sculpt the character
* Children can make a Shivering Shake

Five Jars on the Shelf

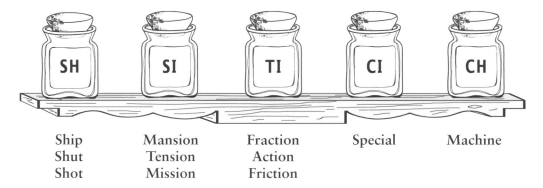

SH	SI	TI	CI	CH
Ship	Mansion	Fraction	Special	Machine
Shut	Tension	Action		
Shot	Mission	Friction		

CHATTERING CHERRIES

Read the Story

Upon entering the factory they meet the Chattering Cherries! The Chattering Cherries chime in. However, as they warn the phonics that there is a change in the chatter, all they can say is,
"ch . . . ch . . . ch . . . ch . . . ch . . ."

Projects

* Charade this sound by using your hands to open and close going "ch, ch"
* Sculpt the character

Two Jars on the Shelf

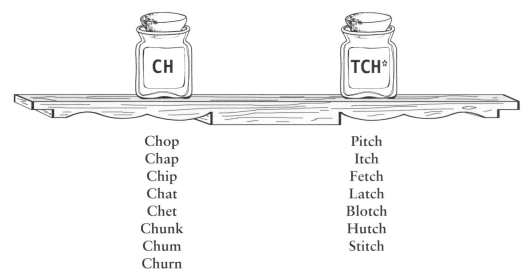

Chop	Pitch
Chap	Itch
Chip	Fetch
Chat	Latch
Chet	Blotch
Chunk	Hutch
Chum	Stitch
Churn	

* TCH is preceded by a short vowel sound

Dictation

Chip had a chat.

OODLES OF OOZE

Read the Story

Everywhere they found Oodles of Ooze! Oops! It was oozing out of everything! A fearful food fight had begun! Oodles fell on the factory doodles just south of the factory poodles. All over the factory all you could hear was, "OO . . . OO . . . OO . . . OO . . . OO . . ."

Projects

- Reinforce this sound by using a tube of icing and cover it with a label that says, "Oodles of Ooze"
- Say: Cool Carrot, Oodles of Ooze, Leaping Lemonade. What's the word? "cool"
- Charade this character squeezing a tube of imaginary ooze
- Sculpt the character

Mnemonic Reading and Writing, Sculpting, Charading, and Painting

1. Too: Tumbling Tomato, Oodles of Ooze.
2. Zoo: Zipping Zucchini, Oodles of Ooze.
3. Coo: Cool Carrot, Oodles of Ooze.
4. Pool: Popping Popcorn, Oodles of Ooze, Leaping Lemonade.

5. Blue: Beautiful Banana, Leaping Lemonade, Oodles of Ooze ("ue").
6. True: Tumbling Tomato, Racing Raisins, Oodles of Ooze ("ue").
7. Glue: Galloping Gumdrop, Leaping Lemonade, Oodles of Ooze ("ue").
8. Flue: Fancy Fish, Leaping Lemonade, Oodles of Ooze ("ue").
9. Chew: Chattering Cherries, Oodles of Ooze ("ew").
10. New: Napping Noodle, Ooodles of Ooze) ("ew").
11. Dew: Dancing Doughnut, Oodles of Ooze ("ew).
12. Crew: Cool Carrot, Racing Raisin, Oodles of Ooze ("ew").
13. You: Yodleing Yams, Oodles of Ooze (spelled "ou").
14. Soup: Singing Sundae, Oodles of Ooze Popping Popcorn ("ou").
15. Youth: Yodeling Yams, Oodles of Ooze, Thirsty Thermos ("ou").
16. Group: Galloping Gumdrop, Racing Raisin, Oodles of Ooze Popping Popcorn ("ou").

If the children can correctly sound blend the words, squeeze out a tiny bit of Oodles of Ooze for them. Repeat the same procedure for all the jars on the shelf.

Four Jars on the Shelf

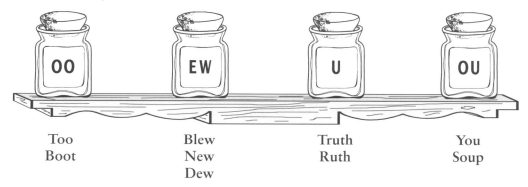

OO	EW	U	OU
Too	Blew	Truth	You
Boot	New	Ruth	Soup
	Dew		

Dictation

It was too hot.
He blew on the soup.

OOKIE COOKIE

Read the Story

The Ookie Cookie had been zapped! There was ook everywhere! Behind every nook was ook! On every cookie was ook! Everyone was looking at the ook! Everyone was saying,
"oo . . . oo . . . oo . . . oo . . . oo . . ."

Projects

• To charade this character hold your hands at your sides as if offered something you don't want saying "oo."

Mnemonic Reading and Writing, Sculpting, Charading, and Painting

1. Cook: Cool Carrot, Ookie Cookie, King Kiwi.
2. Good: Galloping Gumdrop, Ookie Cookie, Dancing Doughnut.
3. Book: Beautiful Banana, Ookie Cookie, King Kiwi.
4. Hook: Hammering Hot Dog, Ookie Cookie, King Kiwi.
5. Put: Popping Popcorn, Ookie Cookie, Tumbling Tomato (spelled "u").

THEN THERE WERE THOUSANDS — THOUSANDS OF THINGS

Read the Story

Then there were thousands of things. Thousands of things everywhere! Then we heard the sound of them, resounding to the path.
"th . . . th . . . th . . . th . . . th . . ."

"Th" can be pronounced as "th" as in the word "then" or "thus." It also can be pronounced as in the word "thirsty."

The importance of this story is to differentiate between "then there were thousands" and the upcoming "Thirsty Thermos."

Projects

- "Then there were thousands of things" is charaded by the pouring of things out of a jar
- You can use the multi-colored sprinkles that come in a little jar in the baking department for a special treat

Word List

1. This
2. Then
3. That
4. Thus
5. Them
6. There
7. Either

Dictation

Then, either pick this or that.

ARTISTIC ARTICHOKE

Read the Story

Artistic Artichoke was in the middle of an art lesson, singing an aria under an arch when he was zapped! The ooze felt like tar! Artistic Artichoke flung it far, up to a star! All he could say was,
"ar . . . ar . . . ar . . . ar . . . ar . . ."

Projects

- Charade by pretending to flip a paintbrush in your hand
- Give a treat of a baby artichoke
- Sculpt the character
- Make up stories about artists
- Say: Artistic Artichoke, Tumbling Tomato. What's the word? "art"

Mnemonic Reading and Writing, Sculpting, Charading, and Painting

1. Art: Artistic Artichoke, Tumbling Tomato.
2. Arm: Artistic Artichoke, Muscular Mushroom.
3. Ark: Artistic Artichoke, King Kiwi.
4. Yard: Yodeling Yams, Artistic Artichoke, Dancing Doughnut.
5. Smart: Singing Sundae, Muscular Mushroom, Artistic Artichoke, Tumbling Tomato.
6. Scarf: Singing Sundae, Cool Carrot, Artistic Artichoke, Fancy Fish.
7. Dart: Dancing Doughnut, Artistic Artichoke, Tumbling Tomato.
8. Yarn: Yodeling Yam, Artistic Artichoke, Napping Noodle.
9. Gargle: Galloping Gumdrop, Artistic Artichoke, Galloping Gumdrop, Leaping Lemonade.
10. Farm: Fancy Fish, Artistic Artichoke, Muscular Mushroom.

Note the "ar" sound is one sound even though it is spelled with two letters. Example: Artistic Artichoke, Muscular Mushroom spells "arm."

WHINING WHEAT CRACKER

Read the Story

Whining Wheat Cracker did not know where to go!
What made this happen . . . ?
When did this happen . . . ?
Where did this come from . . . ?
Why did this happen . . . ?
She whined and whined and whined,
"wh . . . wh . . . wh . . . wh . . . wh . . ."

Projects

- Charade this word by pretending to wipe the tears from your eyes
- Say "wh" as if you were blowing out a candle

Sample words: When, Where, Why, Which.

Mnemonic Reading and Writing, Sculpting, Charading, and Painting

1. Which: Whining Wheat Cracker, Inedible Insect, Chattering Cherries.
2. When: Whining Wheat Cracker, Entertaining Eggs, Napping Noodle.
3. Whip: Whining Wheat Cracker, Inedible Insect, Popping Popcorn
4. Why: Whining Wheat Cracker, (long "I" spelled "y").
5. Whim: Whining Wheat Cracker, Inedible Insect, Muscular Mushroom.
6. Whopper: Whining Wheat Cracker, Ominous Olive, Popping Popcorn, Racing Raisins ("er").
7. What: Whining Wheat Cracker, Upside-Down Cake (spelled **a**), Tumbling Tomato.

Special Three-syllable Word

"Whenever." Discuss and clap out the syllables. Say: "First syllable, Whining Wheat Cracker, Entertaining Eggs, Napping Noodle. Second syllable, Entertaining Eggs, Vested Vegetables. Third syllable, Racing Raisin (spelled "er")."

DRIPPING DRESSING

Read the Story

I will sing to you with a ring! We are about to discover everything! To the treasure chest we will swing! Ring-a-ding-ding! This is just the thing!

Dripping Dressing said, "Oh me! It is not as sad as it could be! Open your eyes and you will see that I have found the 'Treasure Key!' "
"ng . . . ng . . . ng . . . ng . . . ng . . ."

Projects

- Charade this sound by appearing to be dripping with dressing
- Sculpt the character
- Make up stories

Word List

1. Singing
2. Banging
3. Ringing
4. Bringing
5. Longing
6. Stinging
7. Hanging
8. Swinging

OILY OYSTERS

Read the Story

The Oily Oysters thought they had escaped the food fight. . . . Boy, were they foiled! It felt like oil! In their toil from the oil all they could do was point and say, "oy . . . oy . . . oy . . . oy . . . oy . . ."

Projects

- Charade this sound by holding your hands out to the sides bent up and say, "oy, oy, oy"
- Print "Oily Oysters" in large print. Children can draw another picture inside the **O**s

There are two spellings for this sound: "oy" and "oi."

Two Jars on the Shelf

Boy
Joy

Oil

Mnemonic Reading and Writing, Sculpting, Charading, and Painting

1. Boy: Beautiful Banana, Oily Oysters ("oy").
2. Toy: Tumbling Tomato, Oily Oysters ("oy").
3. Joy: Juggling Jellybean, Oily Oysters ("oy").
4. Coy: Cool Carrot, Oily Oysters ("oy").
5. Ploy: Popping Popcorn, Leaping Lemonade, Oily Oysters ("oy").
6. Soy: Singing Sundae, Oily Oysters ("oy").
7. Oil: Oily Oysters Leaping Lemonade ("oi").
8. Toil: Tumbling Tomato, Oily Oysters, Leaping Lemonade ("oi").
9. Join: Juggling Jellybean, Oily Oysters, Napping Noodle.
10. Joint: Juggling Jellybeans, Oily Oysters (spelled "oi"), Napping Noodle, Tumbling Tomato.
11. Coil: Cool Carrot, Oily Oysters, (spelled "oi") Leaping Lemonade.
12. Boil: Beautiful Banana, Oily Oysters (spelled "oi"), Leaping Lemonade.

Review that "oy" and "oi" are one sound but two letters. The spelling of "oi" is used in the medial position of most words and the spelling "oy" is used at the end of words.

THIRSTY THERMOS

Read the Story

Thirsty Thermos was so thirsty! He had such a sore throat! Thirsty Thermos was thrilled to find a thin thimbleful of water. He said, "I just need three drinks of this."

"th . . . th . . . th . . . th . . . th . . ."

Projects

- Charade the sound by pretending to take a drink of water
- Sculpt the sound

Practice List

1. Thrash
2. Thin
3. Bath
4. Thing
5. Path
6. Ether

OUNCES OF OUCH

Read the Story

Just then Ounces of Ouch slid by out of control! The pet cat pounced on a mouse. They were as loud and outlandish as could be. As the mouse was ousted, all you could hear was,

"ow . . . ow . . . ow . . . ow . . . ow . . ."

Projects

- Charade the sound as if you were falling over saying "ow, ow, ow"
- Act out the story
- Tell original cat and mouse stories

Word List

1. Ouch
2. Out
3. Pout
4. Mouth
5. Ground
6. Found
7. Proud
8. Shout
9. Grouch
10. Couch

Dictation

The grouch shouted ouch!

The spelling "ow" is mainly used in the medial position.

1. Owl
2. Clown
3. Cow
4. Sow
5. Brown
6. How
7. Fowl
8. Vow
9. Prowl
10. Crown

Dictation

The clown had a crown that was brown.

MISS SCHWA

Read the Story

Miss adorable Schwa is about to agree to tell of her ability. She can transform, but all she can say is "u" and you'll only find her hiding in the dictionary, as she disguises herself as a, e, i, o, u. By the way, she also likes to share her secret sound with Upside-Down Cake!

"u . . . u . . . u . . . u . . . u . . ."
(∂)   (∂)   (∂)   (∂)   (∂)   (pronounced "uh")

Tell the children that the only place they will find Miss Schwa is in the dictionary. She is the upside-down **e**.

Projects

- Charade Miss Schwa by pointing over your shoulder and say the sound of **u** (short **u**). Both the short **u** sound and the schwa sound are pronounced the same way
- Hide face with hands
- For a food, 7-Up may be used but call it "5-Up" for the five sounds

Practice Schwa

"A" for schwa is in the words "around," "banana, "about," "a," "an," "and."
"E" for schwa is in the words "loaded," "eaten," "mitten."
"I" for schwas is in the words "unity," Emily."
"O" for schwa is in the words "wagon," "collect."
"U" for schwa is in the word "faithful."

AWFUL ALLSPICE

Read the Story

Aw! It was Awful Allspice causing all the awesome trouble! He was awestruck. All everyone could say was, "This was awful!"
"aw . . . aw . . . aw . . . aw . . . aw . . .

Six Jars on the Shelf

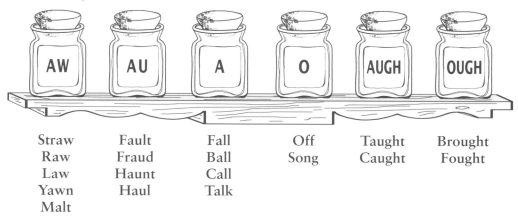

AW	AU	A	O	AUGH	OUGH
Straw	Fault	Fall	Off	Taught	Brought
Raw	Fraud	Ball	Song	Caught	Fought
Law	Haunt	Call			
Yawn	Haul	Talk			
Malt					

THE TREASURE CHEST

Read the Story

The phonics left the factory and the food fight behind them! They were on their way to the treasure chest. Dripping Dressing inserted the key; inside was a secret message!

"Here lies the secret. Join your phonics to my vowels and you will be able to read words with delight! Just remember, my letters say their names and most words will be easy to read. The secret letters are A, E, I, O, U! If you can decode the hidden words, you have found the treasure!"

LONG A

The secret word is — "cake"! (Long "a" is a piece of cake.)

The Secret Scroll for the Long A Vowel

The long vowel sounds combine with the phonics to make vowel sounds that say their own name. The long **a** vowel says **a**. Can you decode the secret word?

C, (long) **a, k,** (magic **e**). "Cake."

Seven Jars on the Shelf

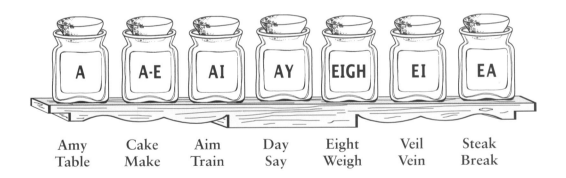

A	A-E	AI	AY	EIGH	EI	EA
Amy	Cake	Aim	Day	Eight	Veil	Steak
Table	Make	Train	Say	Weigh	Vein	Break

LONG E

The secret word is — "beet"! (Long "e" is a sweet beet.)

The Secret Scroll for the Long E Sound

Can you sound blend the secret word for the long e sound?
B, ee, t.
Say it fast: "Beet."

Ten Jars on the Shelf

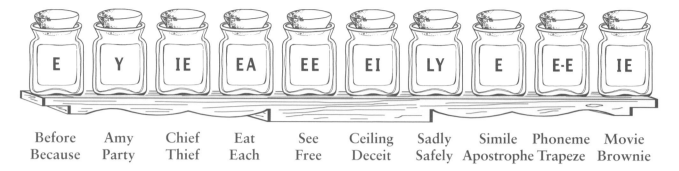

E	Y	IE	EA	EE	EI	LY	E	E·E	IE
Before	Amy	Chief	Eat	See	Ceiling	Sadly	Simile	Phoneme	Movie
Because	Party	Thief	Each	Free	Deceit	Safely	Apostrophe	Trapeze	Brownie

LONG I

The secret word is — "pie"! (Long "i" is a slice of pie.)

The Secret Scroll for the Long "I" Sound

Can you decode the secret word for the long "i"?
"P," "ie."
Say it fast: "Pie."

Six Jars on the Shelf

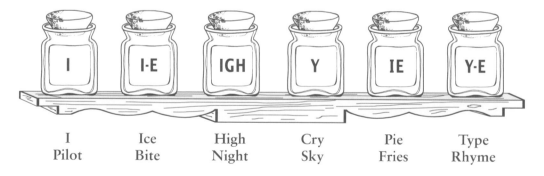

I	I·E	IGH	Y	IE	Y·E
I	Ice	High	Cry	Pie	Type
Pilot	Bite	Night	Sky	Fries	Rhyme

LONG O

The secret word is — "oats"! (Long "o" is a bowl of oats.)

The Secret Scroll for the Long O Sound

"Oa," t, s.
Say it fast: "Oats."

Five Jars on the Shelf

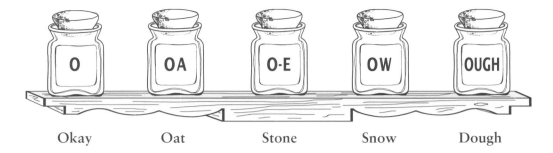

O	OA	O-E	OW	OUGH
Okay	Oat	Stone	Snow	Dough

LONG U

The secret word is — "cube"! (Long "u" is a cute cube.)

The Secret Scroll for the Long U Sound:

C, u, b (magic e).
Say it fast: "Cube."

Six Jars on the Shelf

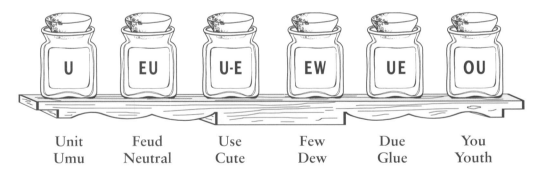

U	EU	U-E	EW	UE	OU
Unit	Feud	Use	Few	Due	You
Umu	Neutral	Cute	Dew	Glue	Youth

THE TREASURE

You have found the treasure — the secret of reading. You will have fun and excitement discovering how wonderful reading can be.

SECRET RECIPE MIX

A magical wand for magical "e." If you add "e" to the end of a short "i" syllable word, you can make the vowel say its name.

You can turn man into mane; pet into Pete; bit into bite; cub into cube.

Toward a Whole New World

(Not in children's book)

As the phonics proceeded past the treasure chest, they entered a whole new world. The first adventure they experienced is a gate that talked to them. It said, "You must first ask a question for me to open." The phonics got together and asked, "Is this the way to reading new words?" The gate responded that it was and quickly opened.

As they walked along the path, they found secret messages. The messages read,

- Do you have an idea?
- Can you tell us the details and main ideas of your thoughts?
- Can you organize your thoughts?
- Do you plan with a beginning, middle and end?
- Can you speak in sentences that have a complete thought?
- Can you put together a group of sentences about the same thought to form a paragraph?
- Can you use a narrative hook to grab the reader's attention?
- Can you indent your paragraphs?
- Do your words flow and create wonderful images?

The last message they found read, "If you can do all of the above, we would like you to become an author of adventure stories. We want you to write stories for other children to read and enjoy. We want you to share the secret with them that you have found along this path.

Reading and the World of Computers

A culminating project can be the use of the computer to reinforce all of the previous learning. Children can create their own stories to be transferred to a computer.

The students can create stories with a beginning, middle, and end. They can select a few of the characters and write an adventure. Younger children can just select the characters.

Select a graphics/media program (there are many on the market). The characters may be scanned into the program. Sculpted characters could be photographed with a digital camera and transferred to the computer program.

The children's stories may be produced by using several cards or "sticky notes" and typed or read into the computer program. Sounds and/or sound effects may also be used making the story come alive. Concepts and skills are thus reinforced.

Appendices

A. Charade List

B. Sculpting, Writing Stories, Acrylic Paintings

C. Sculpting Directions

D. Using Books to Develop Reading Enjoyment and Phonemic Awareness

E. Story Page Model

F. Certificate of Achievement

G. Parent/Teachers' Phonemic Awareness Observation Record

Appendices E, F, and G
may be reproduced for your use.

APPENDIX A

Charade List:

Aa   Hands brush off ants. (Antsy Apple)

Bb: Bounce ball. (Beautiful Banana)

Cc: Snap fingers. (Cool Carrot)

Dd: Move arms and hands as if dancing.(Dancing Doughnut)

Ee: Flip hand palm side up.(Entertaining Eggs)

Ff: Make a flutter movement with hands (Fancy Fish)

Gg: Pretend to be on a horse holding reins. (Galloping Gumdrop)

Hh.   Hold a hammer and hammer. (Hammering Hot Dog)

Ii: Act as though pushing away a plate. (Inedible Insects)

Jj: Juggle balls in the air. (Juggling Jellybeans)

Kk: Make a kicking motion. (King Kiwi)

Ll: Spread arms as if leaping. (Leaping Lemonade)

Mm: Flex arms to make muscles. (Muscular Mushroom)

Nn: Place head on shoulder and close eyes. (Napping Noodle)

Oo: Pretend to hold up cape in front of face. (Ominous Olives)

Pp: Make popping effect with fingers snapping in the air. (Popping Popcorn)

Qq: Hand shaking while making a pouring motion. (Quivering Quake)

Rr: Pretend to be shifting gears in a race car. (Racing Raisin)

Ss: Hold up a pretend tray in the air. (Singing Sundae)

Tt: Movement as if tumbling. (Tumbling Tomato)

Uu: Arms in air as if falling. (Upside-Down Cake)

Vv: Hold onto an imaginary vest. (Vested Vegetables)

Ww: Make a splashing effect as if wallowing. (Wallowing Waffles)

Xx: Pretend to open a pop can. (X-Soda)

Yy: Hands to mouth to pretend to yodel. (Yodeling Yams)

Zz: Make a zipping motion. (Zipping Zucchini)

Ss: Open a treasure chest. (Treasure Chest)

Sh: Put finger up to mouth as if to say "sh." (Shivering Shake)

Ch: Make fingers move quickly as if chattering to each other. (Chattering Cherries)

OO: Squeeze a tube of imaginary ooze. (Oodles of Ooze)

oo: Hands at sides as if shaking off saying "oo." (Ookie Cookie)

Th: Make a pouring motion. (Thousands of Things)

Ar:　　　Make a flipping motion with an imaginary paintbrush. (Artistic Artichoke)

Wh:　　Wipe away tears as if whining. (Whining Wheat Cracker)

ng:　　　Put key in lock (ending sound). (Dripping Dressing)

Oy:　　　Hold hands up with bent elbow as though balancing. (Oysters)

Th:　　　Pretend to be taking a drink of water. (Thirsty Thermos)

Ow:　　Act as if falling down. (Ounces of Ouch)

Schwa sound:　Point over shoulder and say the sound of a short "u." (Miss Schwa)

Aw:　　Hands at sides, looking down. (Awful Allspice)

If you charade a word with a long vowel sound, you just say the long vowel sound and the spelling, i.e., day — dancing doughnut (long "A" spelled "ay").

APPENDIX B

Sculpting Characters with Clay

Materials needed: 1–2 sets of multi-colored clay,
                       toothpicks for use as clay tools,
                       and a toaster-oven or 275-degree oven

The sculpted characters can be quite small. They can be created to be three dimensional or flat. Clay can be separated and grouped by colors for each student ahead of time. Plastic wrap works well and clay can be quickly and easily distributed. Each character's details can be made by forming "balls" or "snakes." The short vowel sound characters can have their mouths shaped to say their sound with a pencil or toothpick. Step by step simple instructions along with teacher demonstration will help ensure student success. Toothpicks make great clay tools and pieces need to be attached to the character creations securely by scoring the edges. If you are using a product such as Sculpey™, bake the clay characters at 250–275 degree in an oven or toaster-oven for six to ten minutes. Watch carefully! The clay may discolor or burn if baked too hot or too long.

Working with small details is a great way to develop gross and fine motor skills in all children. You will be amazed at how well they will do!

Writing Stories

Materials needed: 6x9 inch paper
                       Pencils
                       Colored markers
                       6x9 inch fluorescent or fun paper

Students can make and write or dictate stories about their favorite characters. 8½" × 11" inch white paper should be folded in half and stacked on top of colored cover paper. A staple or two down the crease will hold the pages together. Concepts as simple as beginning, middle, and end can be introduced, practiced, and assessed. The teacher may want to have her very young students dictate their story. Students can trace over the letters and words with a pencil or marker. Illustrations can be drawn in pencil first and traced with a marker. Color can be added to their drawings. A flat clay character can be attached to the cover with hot glue as a finishing touch.

Acrylic Paintings

Materials needed: Canvas boards, 5x7 or smaller,
acrylic brushes, 1/4 inch, fan, and
detail small jars of acrylic paint: white
black, cadmium green, hooker's
green, red, yellow, cerulean blue,
raw and burnt sienna.

Water containers, paper towels,
Paint shirts

Painting is most successful when working in small groups of 2–5 students. Acrylic paint will not wash out of clothes or brushes once it has dried, but it adds permanency and meaning to a student's creation. Blending and mixing techniques can be taught as well as color theory; primary plus primary make secondary colors, tint, tone, and shade, etc. Begin with the cerulean blue and white. Paint the blue on for the sky and tint with white to lighten the sky down towards the horizon. White and black can be mixed to make a gray, and mountains can be painted with white highlights for snow. Both greens can be used to paint a middleground and foreground. When this dries students can paint scenes from adventure stories.

APPENDIX C

Aa

Ff

Bb

Gg

Cc

Hh

Dd

Ii

Ee

Jj

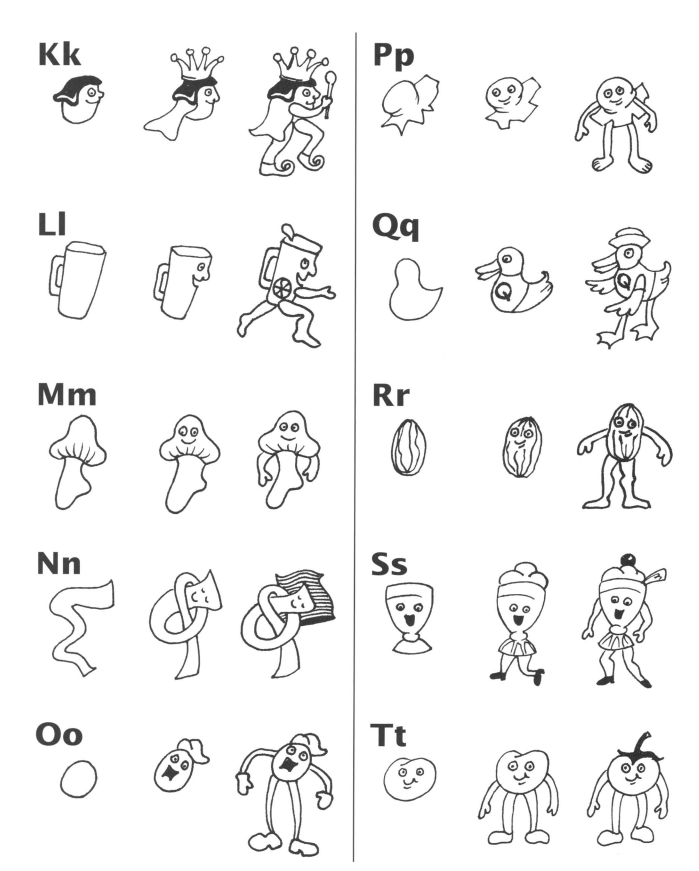

Kk

Ll

Mm

Nn

Oo

Pp

Qq

Rr

Ss

Tt

Uu

Vv

Ww

Xx

Yy

Zz

sh

ch

OO

oo

th

ar

wh

ng

oy

th

ow

∂

aw

APPENDIX D

Using Books to Develop Reading Enjoyment and Phonemic Awareness

1. Read the book to the children for enjoyment.

2. Read the book and stop when you come to a rhyming word. Ask the children to state which word might fit.

3. Ask the children to tell you another word that begins with the same sound as the given word.

4. Tell or ask the children what the author is doing with the words. "The author is changing the first part in some of these words. She then uses the word three times. Can you hear it?" If you want to determine if the children notice this on their own, you might ask, "What's the author doing with some of these words?"

5. Allow for spontaneous responses. A child may chime in with words, want to dramatize some or all of the story, or create another similar story. All of these responses are appropriate and will further help the children to sense that reading is a pleasurable activity.

The Adventures of

_____

Written by

_____

Illustrated by

_____

has successfully completed the

Fantastic Phonics
Food Factory!

Parent/Teachers' Phonemic Awareness Observation Record

Child's name _____

Date	Title of book	States words that rhyme; states other rhyming words	Hears and states sound at the start of a word	States another word that begins with the same sound as a given word	Other observations

BIBLIOGRAPHY

Adams, M. *Beginning to Read: Thinking and Learning about Print*, a summary. Urbana, IL: Center for the Study of Reading, University of Illinois. 1990.

Allen, L. "An Integrated Strategies Approach: Making Word Identification Instruction Work for Beginning Readers." The Reading Teacher, 52 (1998): 254–268.

Barr, R. "Beginning Reading Instruction: from Debate to Reformation," in P. D. Pearson, et al, *Handbook of Reading Research*. White Plains, NY: Longman. 1984.

Bear. D. et al, *Words Their Way: Word Study for Phonics, Vocabulary, and Spelling Instruction*. Columbus, OH: Merrill. 1996.

Bond. G. & Dykstra, R. "The Cooperative Research Program in First-Grade Reading Instruction," *Reading Research Quarterly*, 2 (1967).

Darling-Hammond, L. *Doing What Matters Most: Investing in Quality Teaching*. New York: National Commission on Teaching and America's Future. 1997.

Flesch, R. *Why Johnny Can't Read and What You Can Do About It*. New York: Harper & Row. 1955.

Henderson, E. H. *Teaching Spelling*. Boston: Houghton Mifflin. 1985.

Templeton, S. & D. Bear (Eds.). *Development of Orthographic Knowledge and the Foundations of Literacy: A Memorial Festschrift for Edwund H. Henderson*. Hillsdale, NJ: Eribaum. 1992.

Vygotsky, L. S. *Thought and Language*. Cambridge, MA: MIT Press. 1962.

Yopp, H. K. "Developing Phonemic Awareness in Young Children." *The Reading Teacher*, 45 (1992), 696–703.

CHILDREN'S BOOKS TO DEVELOP PHONEMIC AWARENESS

Andrews, S. *Rattlebone Rock*. New York: Harper Trophy. 1997.

Carlson, N. *ABC I Like Mel*. New York: Viking. 1997.

Carlstrom, N. *Better Not Get Wet, Jesse Bear*. New York: Aladdin. 1997.

Ellwand, D. *Emma's Elephant*. New York: Dutton. 1997.

Hamanaka, S. *The Hokey Pokey*. New York: Simon & Schuster. 1997.

Katz, B. *Truck Talk*. New York: Scholastic. 1997.

Lundgren, M. *We Sing the City*. New York: Clarion. 1997.

Mallett, D. *Inch by Inch*. New York: Harper Trophy. 1997.

Medearis, A. *Rum-a-Tum-Tum*. New York: Holiday House. 1997.

Mora, P. *Uno, Dos, Tres; One, Two, Three*. New York: Clarion. 1997.

Most, B. *Moo-Ha*. San Diego, CA: Harcourt. 1997.

Roberts, B. *Camel Caravan*. New York: Tambourine. 1996.

Sturges, P. *What's That Sound, Wooly Bear?* Boston: Little, Brown. 1996.

Shar Wilkes

Shar Wilkes grew up in Wilmette, Illinois, and received a Bachelor of Science Degree from the University of Oklahoma. She has attended the National College of Education in Evanston, Illinois, the University of Wyoming, and the University of Wyoming Law School. After twenty-six years of teaching children how to read, Shar Wilkes shares her secrets of the process. Shar is a reading specialist in the Casper Public Schools where she has achieved significant success with her unique method and where she devotes many additional hours working with students for the creation of a newspaper page, "Ink Link" for the *Casper Star Tribune*, a page written by and for students. Shar's love of teaching is reflected in her unselfish commitment and enthusiasm for her students and her profession.

Jane Grogan

Jane Grogan was born in Chicago and spent her childhood years in Connecticut, Pennsylvania, and Minnesota. She received a Bachelor of Arts degree from the University of Wyoming and teaches art in the Casper, Wyoming, school district. Jane is responsible for the creation of the characters and, with Shar, presents workshops and programs for children, parents, and teachers. A "lifetime learner," Jane believes in curriculum integration, excelling in project design and research emphasizing the integration of the visual arts and reading, mathematical concepts, science, and social studies.